AF321598

LIGHT AND SOUND

What makes stuff bright and loud?

Emily Kington

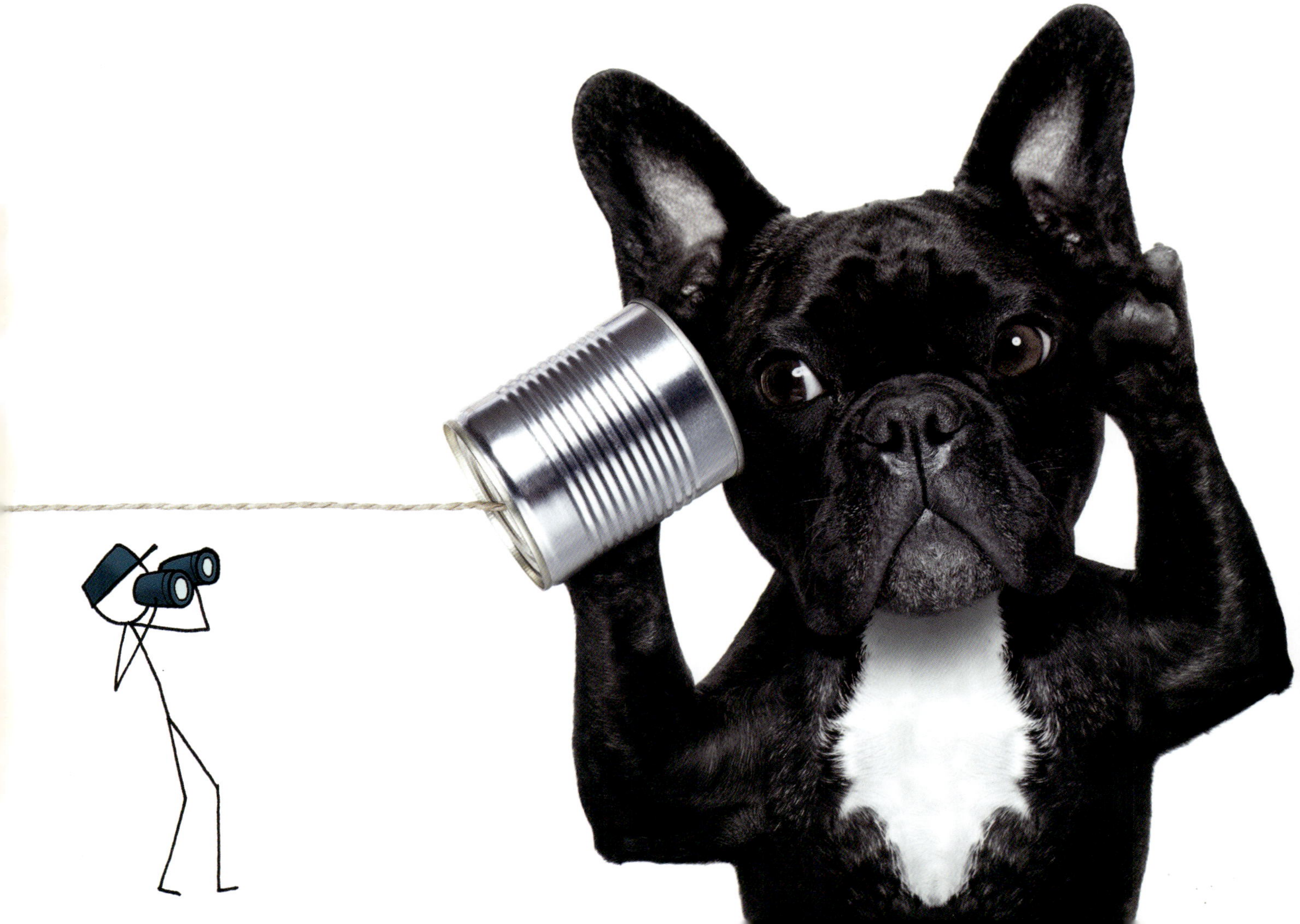

Light allows
us to see.

CONTENTS

Words that appear in **bold** are explained in the glossary.

The answers to the questions are on pages 20–21.

SUNLIGHT

Light is a kind of energy that we see with our **eyes**. During the **day**, we get **natural** light from the sun. We call this light **sunlight**.

NEVER look directly at the sun, even if you are wearing sunglasses, because it can damage your eyes.

Sunlight is very **bright** when there are no **clouds.** Bright light helps us to see things easily.

Clouds in the sky sometimes block some of the sunlight.

Stickmen's Challenge Now it's your turn . . .

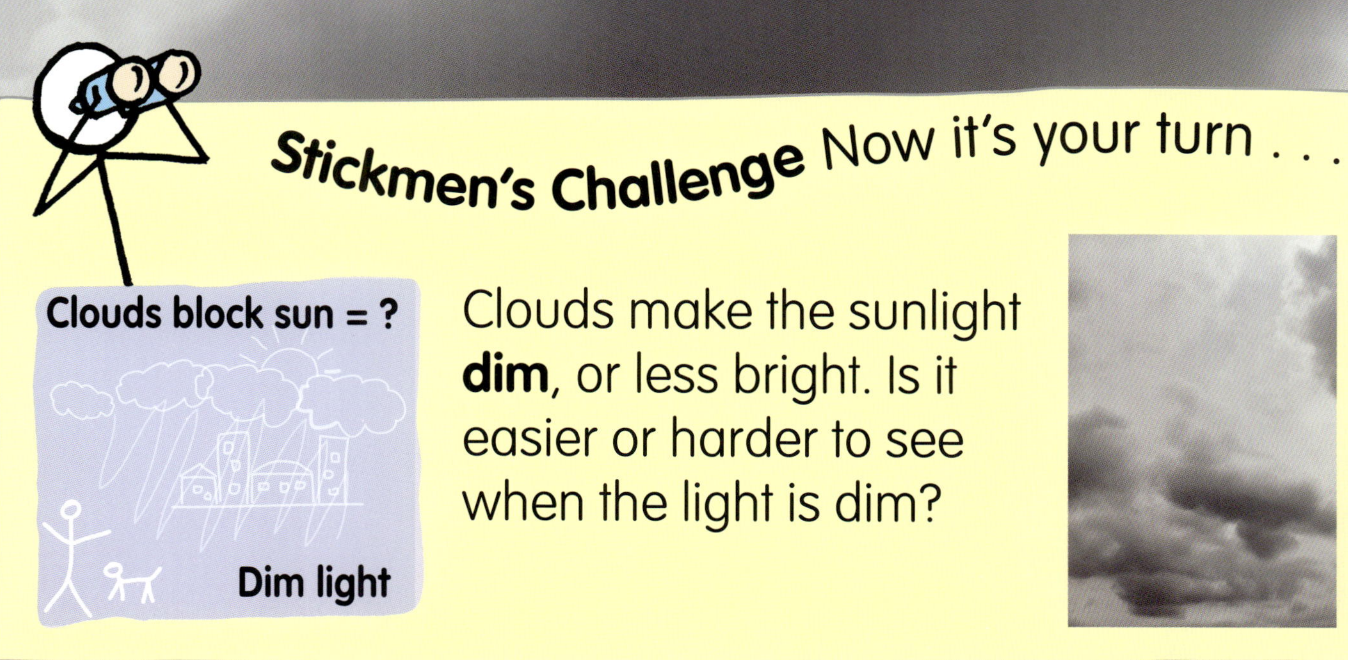

Clouds make the sunlight **dim**, or less bright. Is it easier or harder to see when the light is dim?

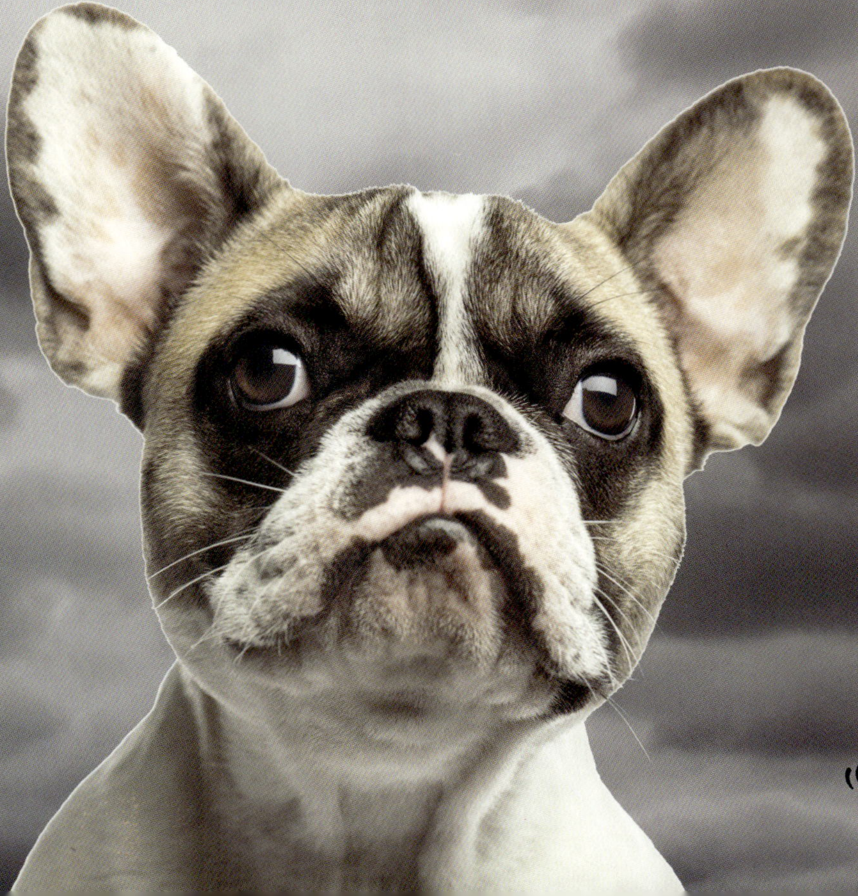

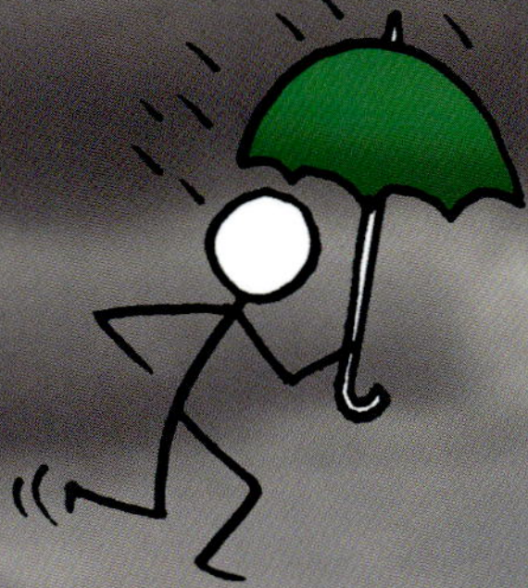

DARKNESS

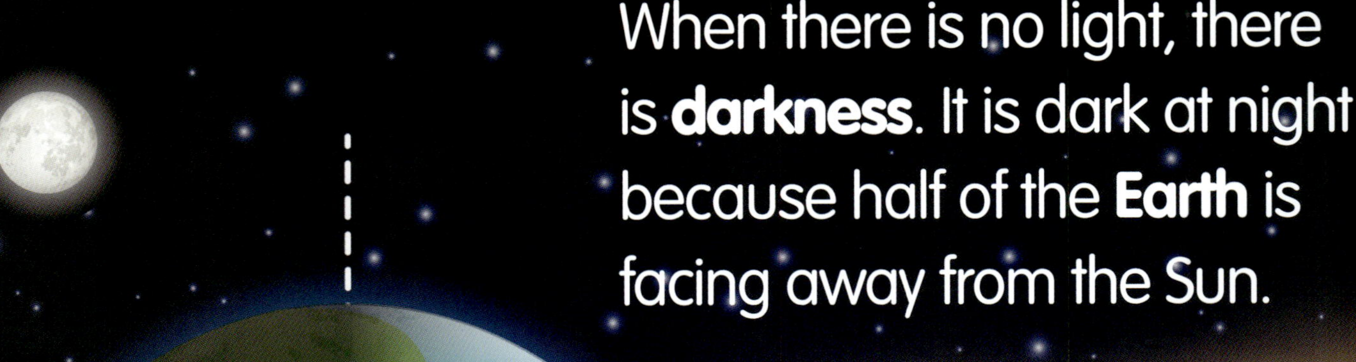

When there is no light, there is **darkness**. It is dark at night because half of the **Earth** is facing away from the Sun.

Earth is a ball that rotates (spins around). It takes 24 hours (or 1 day) to spin all the way around. At any time, half the Earth has sunlight and half is in darkness.

You can block out light with objects that are much smaller than Earth.

MAKING LIGHT

When it is dark, we can make **artificial light** by switching on an electric lamp or a torch.

The light is brightest close to the lamp. The light gets dimmer further away from the lamp.

You can use a lamp or a torch to read in the dark.

Stickmen's Challenge Now it's your turn . . .

Torch close to page

Is it easier or harder to see a page in your book if you hold a torch close to it?

STRAIGHT LINES

Light travels in straight lines. This means we cannot see through walls or around corners.

The lion and ostrich cannot see each other because the wall blocks any light travelling between them.

Do you think the lion and ostrich can see each other if the ostrich looks over the wall?

Light travels in a straight line unless it is blocked.

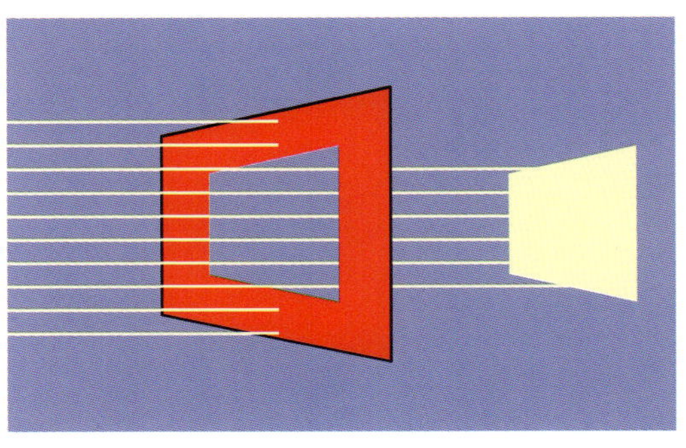

If light shines through a hole, it will keep the same shape as the hole.

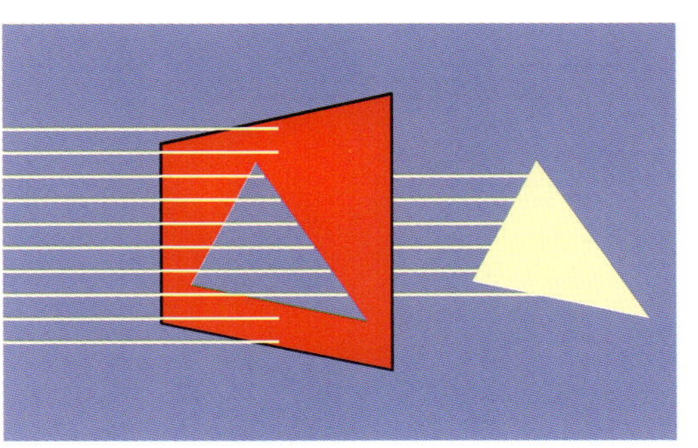

SOUND

Sound is a kind of energy that we hear with our **ears**. Sounds can be **quiet** or loud.

Whispering makes a quiet sound. When we whisper we can only be heard by people near to us.

Stickmen's Challenge Now it's your turn . . .

Shouting is very, very loud if you are near to a person. How loud is it if you are far away?

Shouting makes a loud sound. We shout when we want someone far away to hear us.

VIBRATIONS

Sounds are made of **vibrations** that travel through the **air**. Sounds happen when the air vibrates (moves backwards and forwards very quickly).

We cannot see the vibrations, but when they reach our ears, we hear sounds.

Plucking guitar strings makes them vibrate, which makes sound.

MAKING SOUND

When two objects hit each other, they usually make sound.

Hitting the top of the drum makes it vibrate and produce sound. Hitting the drum gently makes a quiet sound.

Stickmen's Challenge Now it's your turn . . .

A hard hit
BANG!
BANG!

What do you think happens to the sound if you hit the drum harder?

17

HEARD BUT NOT SEEN

Sound travels through the air in a different way than light. Sound is not as easy to block as light.

This cat cannot see the dog around the corner, but it can hear it bark.

You can often hear things that you cannot see.

Stickmen's Challenge Now it's your turn . . .

Will you still be able to hear this fire engine's siren when the fire engine goes around a corner or over a hill?

ANSWERS

Page 5

It is harder to see when the light is dim. Bright light is better for seeing.

Dim light = harder to see

Page 7

It will be dark inside the box because the lid blocks out all the light.

Lid on box = no light in box

Page 9

It is easier to see the page in the dark if you hold the torch close to the book.

Torch close to page = easier to see

Page 11

If the ostrich is looking over the wall, the lion and ostrich can see each other, as the wall is not blocking the line between their eyes.

Ostrich looking over the wall = lion can see the ostrich

Page 13

The shouting sounds quieter, because even loud sounds are quiet if you are far away from them.

Far away = harder to hear

Page 15

The sounds stop when the guitar strings stop vibrating.

No vibrations = no sounds

Page 17

Hitting the drum harder, with increased force, produces louder sounds.

A hard hit = louder sounds

Page 19

You can still hear the fire engine, even when it goes around a corner or over a hill.

Over the hill = heard but not seen

GLOSSARY

air a mixture of gases that are all around us on Earth

artificial light light that is made by humans.

bright strong light that is easy to see

clouds clusters of water droplets that float in the air

darkness when there is no light

day period of daylight from morning to evening

dim weak light that is difficult to see

ears the parts of the body that humans and animals use to hear

Earth the planet where we live. It is a huge, spinning, ball-shaped rock

eyes the parts of the body that humans and animals use to see

light a kind of energy that we see with our eyes

natural made by nature

night period of darkness from evening to morning

quiet little or no sound that is difficult to hear

shouting speaking very loudly

sound a kind of energy that we can hear with our ears

sunlight natural light that comes from the sun

vibrations when something shakes backwards and forwards, or from side to side, very quickly

whispering speaking very quietly

INDEX

Copyright © **2020** Hungry Tomato Ltd

First published in 2020 by Hungry Tomato Ltd

F1, Old Bakery Studios, Blewetts Wharf, Malpas Road, Truro, Cornwall, TR1 1QH, UK

ISBN 978-1-913077-92-1

Printed and bound in China

www.hungrytomato.com

A CIP catalog record for this book is available from the British Library. All rights reserved. No part of this publication may be reproduced, copied, stored in a retrieval system or transmitted in any form or by any means electronic, mechanical, photocopying, recording, or otherwise without prior written permission of the copyright owner.

Picture credits

Shutterstock. 1: Javier Brosch. 2-3: Javier Brosch. 4-5: Sonsedska Yuliia, marigold-y, Eric Isselee, Hollygraphic. 6-7: Siberian Art_GALAXY, Siberian Art, wk1003mike, Javier Brosch. 8-9: sergio34, Artur Synenko , smrm1977, Javier Brosch. 10-11: MaryValery, Andrey_Kuzmin, Issele. 12-13: WilleeCole Photography, Javier Brosc , Lightspring. 14-15: Annette Shaff, Africa Studio , Sonsedska Yuliia. 16-17: Oleg Kozlov, Julia Raketic. 18-19: absolutimages, Le Do, tarubumi.

Every effort has been made to trace the copyright holders, and we apologise in advance for any unintentional omissions. We would be pleased to insert the appropriate acknowledgements in any subsequent edition of this publication.